Cereal MATH

by Karol L. Yeatts

SCHOLASTIC
PROFESSIONAL BOOKS

New York • Toronto • London • Auckland • Sydney
Mexico City • New Delhi • Hong Kong

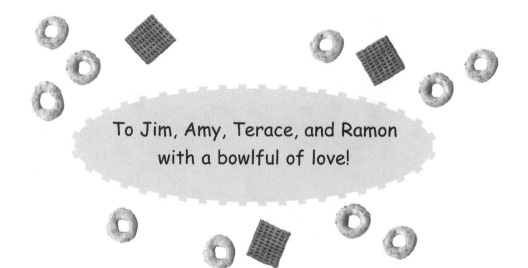

To Jim, Amy, Terace, and Ramon
with a bowlful of love!

Cover design by Norma Ortiz

Interior design by Sydney Wright

Interior illustrations by Cary Pillo

ISBN: 0-590-51208-0

Copyright © 2000 by Karol L. Yeatts

All rights reserved. Printed in the U.S.A.

Contents

Introduction 4

How to Use This Book 5

Connection With the NCTM
Standards 6

Cereal Math Activities

Cereals From A to Z 7
*sequencing cereals alphabetically;
organizing data; counting*

Cereal Day by Day 10
grouping and ordering cereals

Cereal Abacus 13
counting and using fact families

Groups of "O's" 15
counting and grouping by tens

Fruity Places 16
counting and using place value

Two Scoops 19
estimating, counting, and sequencing

A Scrumptious Sort 21
estimating, sorting, and classifying

Cereal Venn Diagrams 23
sorting and classifying using Venn diagrams

Colorful Cereal Patterning 25
creating patterns

Sugar Is Sweet 27
sequencing numbers

Our Favorite Cereal 30
collecting and graphing data

Cereal Stats 32
collecting, graphing, and interpreting data

A, B, C and 1, 2, 3 35
*estimating; collecting, graphing, and
interpreting data*

Measure by Measure 39
measuring length with nonstandard units

A Handful of Cereal 41
measuring area with nonstandard units

How Many Pieces in the Box? 42
measuring weight

Fill 'Er Up! 44
estimating capacity, sequencing

Cereal by the Bowl 46
estimating capacity and comparing volume

Money Matters 47
counting and adding money

Edible Word Problems 50
creating and solving simple word problems

Berry Likely 51
exploring probability

Who Ate the Choco-Bits? 54
using logical reasoning

The New Cereal on the Block 56
*writing a recipe for a new cereal
using fractions*

Shapely Packaging 58
identifying and creating geometric solids

Math Journal reproducible 64

Introduction

I've presented many workshops about using math manipulatives, and I hear the same comment from teachers everywhere: Using manipulatives is wonderful, but adequate funding is not available to purchase these materials. As a result, I began to think of manipulatives that are readily available, economical for teachers, *and* appealing to children. Cereal provided a perfect solution!

Most children have eaten a variety of cereals and are knowledgeable about cereal brands and contents. Since cereal is a natural part of most children's morning routine, it is a motivating "ingredient" to aid in their cognitive development. My goal in writing this book is to present teachers with fun, hands-on activities that use cereal to help children grasp mathematical concepts.

The many colors, sizes, shapes, and textures of cereal provide an excellent means for counting, adding, subtracting, estimating, comparing, sorting, classifying, patterning, and more. Kids will have fun counting and practicing fact families with an easy-to-make cereal abacus. They'll sort fun-shaped cereal by attribute and create colorful patterns. How many raisins are in two scoops? Kids estimate first, then investigate to find out! Several activities in this book integrate measurement by using cereal to explore linear measurement, surface area, and capacity. Experiences in gathering, organizing, displaying, and interpreting data are among the earliest applications of statistics. Children will enjoy collecting and graphing data about favorite cereals, cereal attributes, and more.

All of the activities in this book correlate with the standards recommended by the National Council of Teachers of Mathematics (NCTM). You'll find a chart on page 6 that shows how each activity connects to the NCTM Standards 2000. Using cereal to teach and reinforce math concepts helps make math a treat for kids. I hope that the activities in this book will become a delicious part of your day!

How to Use This Book

The activities covered in this book correspond to the NCTM Standards 2000. Use the handy skills matrix on page 6 to find activities that reinforce a particular standard. The activities are arranged in order of difficulty, beginning with counting and place-value exercises and moving through sorting, graphing, estimating, measuring, and more. Each activity includes the skill or skills at the top of the page, step-by-step how-to's, and "Literature Links." Many activities include reproducible data sheets as well.

Literature Links recommend appealing children's books that provide natural connections to the math concepts covered in each activity. These books can be used to introduce the math activity or as a follow-up extension.

Math Journals are recommended for students to record their observations of the activities. Suggestions for using math journals can be found throughout the activities. The math journal entries can be as simple as recording a guess before actually discovering an answer, or as complex as writing an explanation of the math concept learned. Children can write or draw responses in their math journal depending on their developmental level. You can reproduce the Math Journal sheet on page 64.

Hygiene

Have pre-moistened towelettes or antibacterial hand cleansers for children to wash their hands before working with the cereal.

Safety

It is suggested that you give children cereal to munch that is separate from the cereal used for the activity.

Sources

Ask parents to donate cereal to your class-room. Have tags prepared with cereal requests so that parents can simply pull off the tag and bring it to the grocery store. Ask local grocery stores or supermarkets if they are willing to donate supplies. Many businesses participate in adopt-a-school programs and may be willing to help. The cereals called for in each activity are only suggestions. Feel free to substitute generic-brand cereals or any other kinds of cereals that you think would work.

Food Allergies

Send a note home asking parents about possible food allergies and have substitutes on hand for any allergic children.

Storage

Store cereal in airtight containers or cans, or resealable plastic bags.

Connection With the NCTM Standards 2000

	Numbers and Operation	Estimation*	Number Sense and Numeration*	Concepts of Whole-Number Operations*	Whole-Number Computation*	Fractions and Decimals*	Patterns, Functions, and Algebra	Geometry and Spatial Sense	Measurement	Data Analysis, Statistics, and Probability	Problem Solving	Reasoning and Proof	Communication	Connections	Representation
Cereals from A to Z											●	●	●	●	●
Cereal Day by Day											●	●	●	●	●
Cereal Abacus	●			●	●						●	●	●	●	●
Groups of "O's"	●		●	●	●						●	●	●	●	●
Fruity Places	●		●	●	●						●	●	●	●	●
Two Scoops	●	●	●								●	●	●	●	●
A Scrumptious Sort	●	●	●							●	●	●	●	●	●
Cereal Venn Diagrams	●	●	●							●	●	●	●	●	●
Colorful Cereal Patterning										●	●	●	●	●	●
Sugar Is Sweet	●	●	●	●	●	●	●		●		●	●	●	●	●
Our Favorite Cereal	●		●							●	●	●	●	●	●
Cereal Stats	●	●	●	●	●					●	●	●	●	●	●
A, B, C and 1, 2, 3	●	●	●	●	●			●			●	●	●	●	●
Measure by Measure	●										●	●	●	●	●
A Handful of Cereal	●										●	●	●	●	●
How Many Pieces in the Box?	●	●	●	●	●	●					●	●	●	●	●
Fill 'Er Up!	●	●	●	●	●	●			●		●	●	●	●	●
Cereal by the Bowl	●	●	●								●	●	●	●	●
Money Matters	●	●	●	●	●	●					●	●	●	●	●
Edible Word Problems	●			●	●						●	●	●	●	●
Berry Likely	●									●	●	●	●	●	●
Who Ate the Choco-Bits?											●	●	●	●	●
The New Cereal on the Block	●								●		●	●	●	●	●
Shapely Packaging		●	●					●	●		●	●	●	●	●

*Indicates a subcategory of Numbers and Operation

Cereals From A to Z

Children brainstorm names of cereals, sequence them alphabetically, and organize data on a chart.

aterials

- large chart paper
- pencils
- colored markers
- Cereals from *A* to *Z* chart (page 9)

Cereals from *A* to *Z* chart (page 9)

Getting Ready

Prepare a large *A* to *Z* Chart that is the same as the student *A* to *Z* chart. Give each student a copy of the Cereals from *A* to *Z* chart.

What to Do

1 Ask children how many different kinds of cereal they can name.

2 Have children list cereals that start with each letter of the alphabet. (More than one cereal may be listed for each letter. Some letters do not have any cereals.)

3 When children are finished, they can count the number of cereals they have listed for each letter.

4 Next, have children "pair and share." Working with a partner, children share their lists. They can add any cereals that they did not have on their list.

Teacher Tips

This activity will help students think about different kinds of cereal and will generate interest in using cereal in the classroom.

For younger students, you may wish to complete this activity orally as a group.

Literature Links

Chicka Chicka Boom Boom by Bill Martin Jr. (Simon and Schuster, 1989).

Children will love the bright, bold illustrations of this lively alphabet rhyme. It is a wonderful way to teach or review the letters of the alphabet. After reading the story, children can choose their own alphabet letter and identify a cereal that starts with that letter. For example, *A climbed up to the top of the coconut tree to eat Alpha-Bits®*

5 Share results as a class and write responses on a large wall chart. Children can add to their own charts as well.

Ask children to make up a name for a cereal beginning with a letter that does not have any known cereals.

To extend math learning, have children create a bar graph to show the number of cereals beginning with each letter.

Cereals From A to Z

A	Alpha-Bits	**N**	
B	Bran Flakes	**O**	
C	Cheerios	**P**	
D		**Q**	
E		**R**	
F		**S**	
G		**T**	
H		**U**	
I		**V**	
J		**W**	
K		**X**	
L		**Y**	
M		**Z**	

Cereals From A to Z

A	B	C	D	E	F	G	H	I	J	K	L	M
N	O	P	Q	R	S	T	U	V	W	X	Y	Z

Cereal Day by Day

Children choose a cereal for each day of the week and learn about grouping objects in different orders.

Materials

- @ 7 different variety-sized cereal boxes (4 or 5 of each box, depending on the size of your class)
- @ Cereal Day by Day data sheet (page 12)
- @ pencils
- @ construction paper

Getting Ready

Display seven variety-sized cereal boxes on a table for everyone to see. Make large signs of the days of the week on separate sheets of construction paper. Tape the signs onto the chalkboard in random order.

What to Do

1 Ask a volunteer to arrange the days of the week in correct order, starting with Sunday and ending with Saturday.

2 Explain to children that you must decide which cereal you want to eat for breakfast each day of the week.

3 Pick one of the seven variety-sized cereal boxes and write the name of the cereal next to the Sunday sign. As you write the name of the cereal, say, "On Sunday I am going to eat [Cheerios®] for breakfast."

4 Pick another cereal and write the cereal name next to the Monday sign. Say, "On Monday I am going to eat [Froot Loops®]." Continue until all seven cereal boxes have been matched with a day of the week.

5 Ask children if this is the only way that the boxes of cereal could be arranged. Ask a volunteer to arrange the cereal boxes in a different order.

6 Ask if there are any other ways to arrange the cereal boxes. Choose other volunteers to place the boxes in a new order. (Note that there are actually 5,040 different ways to arrange the seven cereal boxes!)

7 Next, divide the class into groups of seven. (Groups of seven work best, but smaller groups will also work.) Give each group seven different cereal boxes. Give each student a Cereal Day by Day data sheet.

8 Have each child choose a cereal for the first day of the week, Sunday. (Note: Each child will choose a different box. If students wish to choose the same cereal for a given day, tell them that they can choose that cereal for the next day, instead.) Have children record their choice for Sunday on their Cereal Day by Day data sheet.

9 Have children place all the cereal boxes back in the center of the table. Children then choose a different cereal for Monday and record their choice on the data sheet. Continue until a cereal has been chosen for each day of the week.

10 Discuss how each child's Cereal Day by Day data sheet is different from the other children's in their group.

Literature Links

Today Is Monday by Eric Carle (Philomel Books, 1993). This is a delightfully illustrated version of a popular children's song, "Today Is Monday." The verses introduce the reader to the names of the days of the week as the lively animals munch away on their favorite foods. After reading the book, have students create their own "days of the week" mini-book to tell what cereal or food they will eat each day.

Cereal Day by Day

Sunday	
Monday	
Tuesday	
Wednesday	
Thursday	
Friday	
Saturday	

Cereal Math-Scholastic Professional Books

Cereal Abacus

Children practice counting, adding, and subtracting using an easy-to-make cereal abacus. Children learn fact families through hands-on experiences.

aterials

- O-shaped cereal (such as Apple Jacks®)
- pipe cleaners (one per child)
- small paper cups (one per child)
- pencils

Getting Ready

Punch two small holes in the bottom of small paper cups. (The holes should hold a pipe cleaner snugly.) Give each child a paper cup, a pipe cleaner, and at least ten pieces of O-shaped cereal.

What to Do

1. Push one end of the pipe cleaner through one of the holes, so that it extends out the bottom of the cup.

2. Stand the cup upside down and place ten pieces of the cereal on the pipe cleaner.

3. Carefully bend the pipe cleaner in half and poke the other end of the pipe cleaner through the other hole so that it comes out inside the cup.

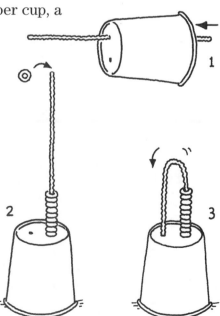

Ten Apples up on Top! by Theo LeSieg (Random House, 1988). This is an engaging story that reinforces counting to ten. The animal characters carefully arrange ten apples on top of their heads. Have children count all the apples on the animals' heads. Counting by tens will be the easiest way to do this.

Annie's One to Ten by Annie Owen (Alfred A. Knopf, 1988). This simple book illustrates all the different combinations of numbers that add up to ten. After reading both books aloud, invite children to illustrate their own fact-families book.

4 Secure the two ends of the pipe cleaner together by wrapping the ends around each other several times. This will keep the pipe cleaner from coming back out of the holes.

Show students how to use the cereal abacus by following these steps:

1 Instruct children to place ten cereal pieces on one side of the abacus.

2 Have children count the cereal as they move one piece at a time to the opposite side of the abacus. Remind children that there are a total of ten pieces of cereal on the abacus.

3 Have children place three pieces of cereal on one side of the abacus. Ask how many pieces are on the other side (7). Review the equation 3 + 7 = 10. Demonstrate several other addition combinations.

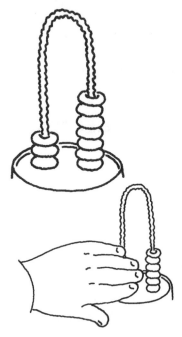

4 Have children place four pieces of cereal on one side of the abacus and then cover the pieces with their hand. Ask how many uncovered pieces of cereal remain (6). Review the equation 10 − 4 = 6. Demonstrate several other subtraction problems.

5 Introduce fact families to children. Have children record a fact family for ten in their math journal. An example of a fact family for ten is:

$$6 + 4 = 10 \qquad 4 + 6 = 10 \qquad 10 - 4 = 6 \qquad 10 - 6 = 4$$

Here's More!

To extend this activity, add more pieces of cereal to the abacus. Have children continue to record fact families in their math journals.

Groups of "O's"

Children use a cereal
counting stick to count by tens.

Materials

- O-shaped cereal (such as Cheerios®)
- pipe cleaners (one per child)   - small paper cups (one per child)

Getting Ready

Give each child a pipe cleaner and a cup holding a small amount of cereal.

What to Do

1 Have children hold their pipe cleaner sideways and place ten pieces of cereal on it.

2 Ask a volunteer to come to the front of the room and count the number of pieces on the pipe cleaner. Explain to children that this represents one group of ten.

3 Ask a second child to come to the front of the room. Explain that there are now two groups of ten, or 20 pieces all together. You may need to count the cereal to show that there are indeed 20 pieces of cereal.

4 Have a third child come up. Ask children how many groups of ten there are now (three groups of ten or 30 pieces.) You may wish to demonstrate how to count by tens at this point.

5 Continue until there are ten children at the front of the room, each with a group of ten pieces of cereal. Count by tens until you have counted all of the children's cereal.

Literature Links

*The Cheerios®
Counting Book*
by Barbara Barbieri
McGrath
(Scholastic Inc.,
1998).
This book uses
Cheerios® to reinforce
the concepts of
grouping and counting
by tens. This is a fun
book to keep in a
counting center with
lots of manipulatives!

Fruity Places

Children practice working with place value as they play a game with colorful cereal place-value cubes.

Materials

- colorful O-shaped cereal (such as Froot Loops®)
- small paper cups
- pipe cleaners
- Styrofoam blocks cut into 6- by 6- by 2-inch blocks (Styrofoam from packing boxes works well. Many craft stores also sell Styrofoam sheets.)
- number cubes (You can use the reproducible on page 18.)
- markers
- construction paper

Getting Ready

Group children into pairs. Give each pair a number cube, a cup of O-shaped cereal, a Styrofoam block, and three pipe cleaners.

What to Do

Demonstrate these steps to make the place-value cubes.

1 Place one end of each of the pipe cleaners into the Styrofoam block.

2 Cut three small labels from construction paper. With a marker, write *hundreds* on one label, *tens* on another, and *ones* on the third.

3 Glue the labels onto the Styrofoam base for each place value stick.

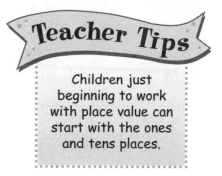

Teacher Tips

Children just beginning to work with place value can start with the ones and tens places.

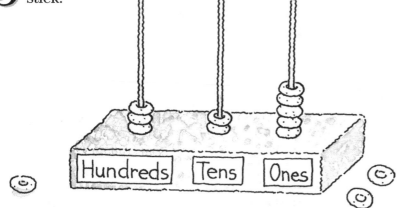

Explain these steps to children to play the game.

1 Player 1 rolls the number cube. He or she places that number of cereal pieces on his or her *ones* place-value stick.
NOTE: You may consider having children use different-colored cereal for each place value to help distinguish them.

2 Player 2 rolls the die and places the corresponding number of cereal pieces on his or her *ones* place-value stick.

3 Players take turns rolling again. This time they place the corresponding number of cereal pieces on the *tens* place-value stick.

4 Players take turns rolling again. This time they place the corresponding number of cereal pieces on the *hundreds* place-value stick.

5 Each player reads his or her number by reading the *hundreds* column, *tens* column, and *ones* column. See the picture above for an example. The player with the greatest number value wins the round.

6 Players remove the cereal and begin round two.

Literature Links

One Hundred Is a Family by Pam Munoz Ryan (Hyperion, 1994). This beautifully illustrated story reinforces counting numbers from 1 to 10 and then by tens to 100.

Number Cubes

Cut along the solid lines.
Fold along the dashed lines.
Tape together to form a cube.

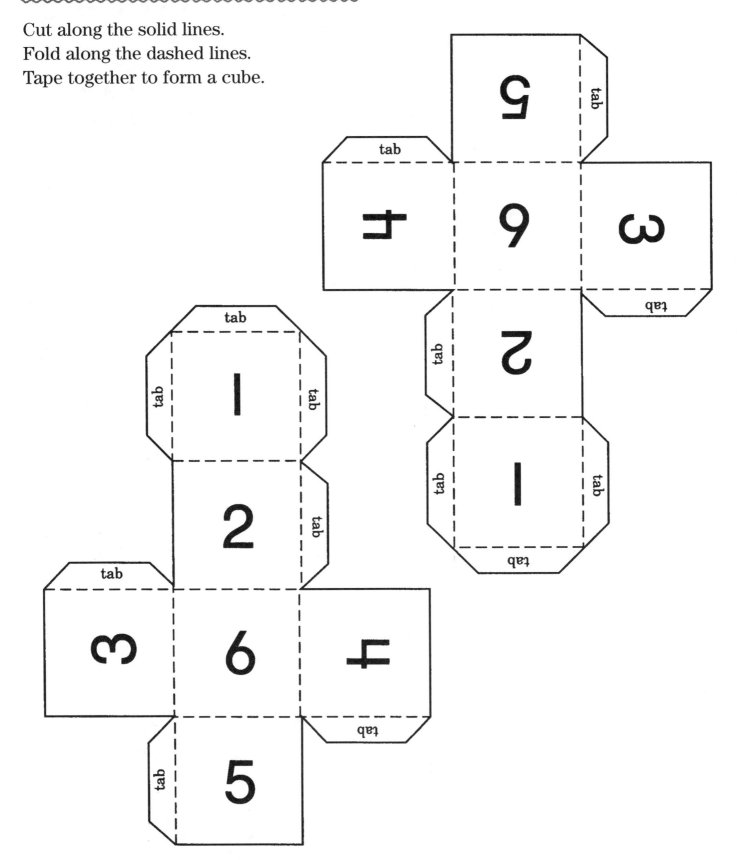

Two Scoops

Children estimate and
find out how many raisins are in a
box of raisin bran cereal.

aterials

- any type of raisin bran or similar cereal
- small paper cups
- small paper squares or self-sticking notes
- sugar scoops
- bowls
- newsprint or paper towels

Getting Ready

Divide a box of raisin bran (or similar cereal) equally among children by giving each child a small cup of cereal. Give each child a bowl, a paper square, and a piece of newsprint or a paper towel.

What to Do

1 Show children the box of cereal and ask them how many raisins they think it contains. Have children record their estimates on a paper square or self-sticking note.

2 Invite children to arrange their estimates in ascending order on the board.

3 Have children pour their cereal onto the newsprint paper and separate the raisins from the rest of the cereal.

4 Ask children to count the number of raisins in their sample and write the number on a paper square.

5 Call on students to tell how many raisins they counted. Write the amounts on the chalkboard.

6 Add the numbers together. Check to see how close children's estimates were to the actual number of raisins counted.

Here's More!

Discuss the advertisement that says there are two scoops of raisins in every box of Raisin Bran®. Ask children if they think this is true. Using a small sugar scoop, scoop up some raisins. Ask a volunteer to count the raisins and record the amount.

Challenge children to figure out how many scoops of raisins are in a box of Raisin Bran®. For example, if there were 80 raisins in a box and a scoop held 20 raisins, then there would be four scoops of raisins in the box. Repeat the steps and discuss the results. Ask questions such as, *Are there the same number of raisins in the second scoop? Did the box have more or less than two scoops of raisins? What are some things that would account for the differences in the results?* (size of raisins, size of the scoop, if the scoop was level or heaping) Have children write their responses in their math journals.

A Scrumptious Sort

Children practice classifying, sorting, and estimating fun-shaped, colorful cereal.

aterials

- multi-shaped, multi-colored cereal (such as Lucky Charms®)
- small paper cups
- pencils
- Sorting Data Sheet (page 22, optional)

Getting Ready

Give each child a small cup of any multi-shaped, multi-colored cereal.

What to Do

1 Ask children if they can name the different shapes and colors that can be found in the box of cereal. Have kids draw the different shapes to make a data sheet. (If using Lucky Charms®, give each student a copy of page 22.)

2 Have children estimate how many of each shape are in their cup of cereal. Have children record their estimates on their Sorting Data Sheet.

3 Next, ask children to sort their cereal on their Data Sheet and count the number of pieces in each group. Have them record the actual number of pieces next to their estimates on the Data Sheet.

4 Provide an opportunity for children to discuss the number of shapes that they have in each category. Have children write or dictate a few sentences describing their sorting. For example:
There were 3 more hearts than I estimated.
I estimated 5 green pieces and I actually had 7 green pieces.
I counted 2 blue pieces and guessed there would be 7.
I did not have any stars.

Literature Links

Math Counts: Sorting by Henry Pluckrose (Children Press, 1995). Children will enjoy discovering how various items in the book have been sorted.

Harriet's Halloween Candy by Nancy Carlson (Puffin/Penguin Books, 1984). Harriet has collected a lot of Halloween candy. Children will enjoy seeing how Harriet sorts her candy, where she hides it, and whether she shares it with her little brother. After reading each story, children can sort items around the classroom, such as crayons, markers, marbles, and so on. They can ask their classmates to guess how they sorted their items.

Sorting
Data Sheet

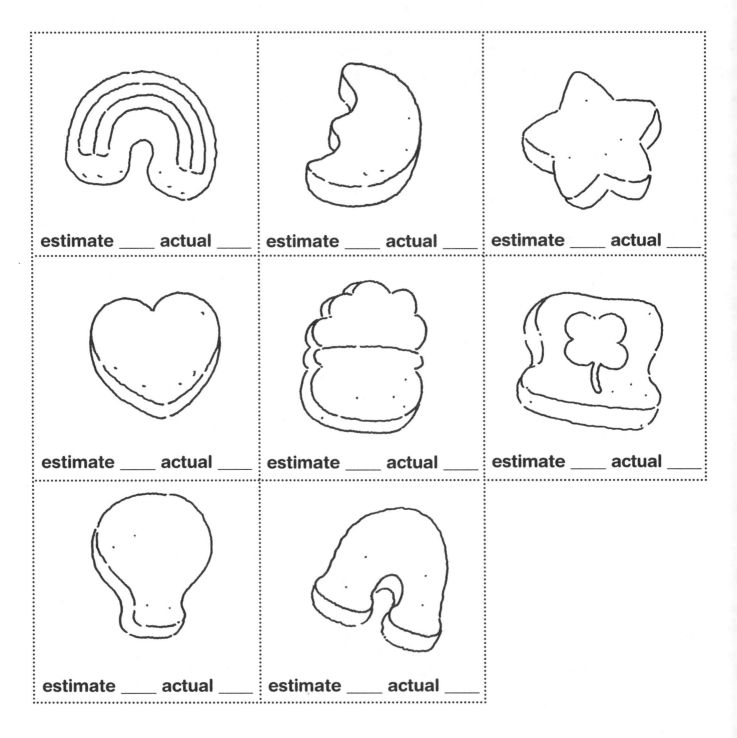

estimate ____ actual ____

estimate ____ actual ____

estimate ____ actual ____

estimate ____ actual ____

estimate ____ actual ____

estimate ____ actual ____

estimate ____ actual ____

estimate ____ actual ____

Cereal Math-Scholastic Professional Books

Cereal Venn Diagrams

Children sort and classify cereal by attributes using Venn diagrams.

Materials

@ 2 kinds of multi-colored, multi-shaped cereal (such as Froot Loops® and Trix®)
@ paper cups
@ two four-foot lengths of yarn or string

Getting Ready

Arrange two overlapping circles of yarn or string on the floor to make a Venn diagram. Pour a small amount of each cereal in a separate paper cup.

What to Do

1 Have children gather around the circle so everyone can see the Venn diagram.

2 Place cereal pieces with a common attribute on one side of the Venn diagram. Have children describe the cereal pieces. (For example, they are all round.)

3 Place cereal pieces with a different common attribute on the other side of the Venn diagram. Have the children describe the cereal pieces. (For example, they are all red.)

4 Find all the cereal pieces that are both round and red and place them in the overlapping section of the Venn diagram.

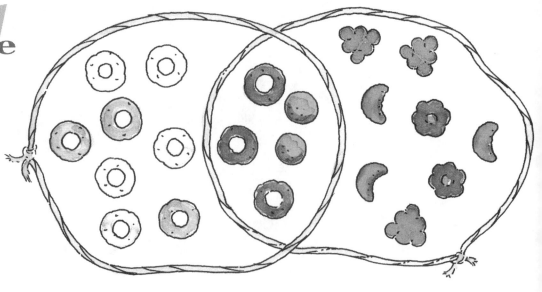

5 Ask children why you placed these pieces in the overlapping part. Help them understand that these cereal pieces share both characteristics: They are all round and red.

6 Repeat the activity with other cereal pieces. Each time, ask children to explain the reason or reasons for the groupings.

Here's More!

Set up a few stations where children can sort cereal in Venn diagrams following the activity steps above.

Colorful Cereal Patterning

> Children create a variety of patterns using colorful pieces of cereal.

aterials

- any multi-colored, multi-shaped cereal (such as Trix®)
- Sorting Data Sheet (page 26, optional)
- small paper cups   - index cards   - glue
- construction paper cut into 3- by 12-inch rectangles

Getting Ready

Give each child a cup of cereal, glue, and a construction-paper rectangle.

What to Do

1. Review the different cereal shapes and have children sort their cereal by shape. Have kids draw the different shapes to make a data sheet. (If using Trix®, give each student a copy of page 26.)

2. Ask children if they know what a pattern is. Explain that a pattern is an order or arrangement that repeats. Give examples of patterns, such as red, blue, red, blue, red, blue.

3. Ask for volunteers to describe a pattern that could be made with the cereal shapes. Then invite children to create their own patterns using their cereal.

4. Have children glue their cereal patterns onto construction paper. When the patterns are thoroughly dry, display them on the bulletin board.

5. Have younger children "read" their patterns by either the shape or color of the cereal pieces. Explain to older children how to read a pattern using letter symbols. (*A* represents the first unit of the pattern, *B* represents a second unit, and so on.)

Literature Links

Math Counts: Pattern by Henry Pluckrose (Children Press, 1995). This book shows a variety of patterns found in the world around children. After reading the story out loud, have children create pattern necklaces using colorful O-shaped cereal and yarn or string. Invite classmates to guess the pattern.

Sorting Data Sheet

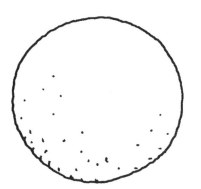

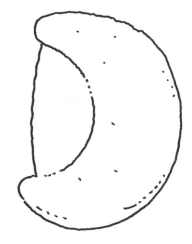

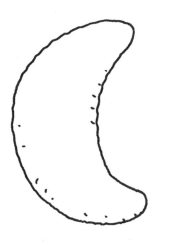

Sugar Is Sweet

Children learn about the sugar content in cereal and arrange cereals from the lowest sugar content to the highest sugar content.

aterials

@ empty cereal boxes (at least ten different types)
@ Sugar Is Sweet Data Sheet (page 29)
@ pencils   @ scissors
@ glue   @ construction paper

Getting Ready

Display the cereal boxes on a table. Give each child a Sugar Is Sweet Data Sheet.

What to Do

1 Show children a cereal box label with the nutrition facts. Ask them if they know what kind of information is found on the label.

2 Write the word *sugar* on the board. Explain that sugar is one of the ingredients in cereal. Also explain that the number next to the word sugar is the amount of sugar per serving. The label also tells you the serving size and how many servings are in a box.

3 Ask the for a volunteer to choose a box of cereal. Ask the child to find out how much sugar per serving is in that cereal.

4 Have the class write the name of the cereal in the first box on their Sugar Is Sweet Data Sheet and the amount of sugar per serving.

Teacher Tips

Using the Nutrition Facts on the side panel of a cereal box, determine how many grams are in one cup of cereal. Show kids what 10 grams looks like. For example, if 1 cup of cereal is 30 grams, fill 1/3 cup to show 10 grams. This will give kids a better understanding of the data they use in this activity.

Note: You will only be recording the amount of sugar per serving size.

Literature Links

Anno's Counting Book by Mitsumasa Anno (HarperCollins, 1977). This wordless picture book introduces the reader to number systems. After sharing the book with children, provide them with a set of number cards to practice arranging the numbers in order.

5 Ask for another volunteer to choose a different box of cereal and to read how much sugar is in one serving.

6 Have the class write the name of the second cereal chosen and the amount of sugar per serving. Continue until all the cereal data has been recorded.

7 Have children cut apart the data boxes.

8 Have children arrange the boxes in order from the least amount of sugar to the greatest amount. Then have them glue their data boxes in order on a piece of construction paper. For example:

Corn Flakes cereal	Froot Loops cereal	Smart Start cereal
2 grams of sugar per serving	12 grams of sugar per serving	13 grams of sugar per serving

Note: Several cereals may have the same amount of sugar. If this occurs, have children place the boxes above one another (this is similar to making a graph).

9 Lead a discussion about the findings. Ask children, *Which cereal has the greatest amount of sugar per serving? Which has the least amount? Which cereals have the same amount of sugar per serving?* You may have children record their questions and answers in their math journals.

Sugar Is Sweet Data Sheet

_____ cereal

_____ grams
of sugar per serving

_____ cereal

_____ grams
of sugar per serving

_____ cereal

_____ grams
of sugar per serving

_____ cereal

_____ grams
of sugar per serving

_____ cereal

_____ grams
of sugar per serving

_____ cereal

_____ grams
of sugar per serving

_____ cereal

_____ grams
of sugar per serving

_____ cereal

_____ grams
of sugar per serving

_____ cereal

_____ grams
of sugar per serving

_____ cereal

_____ grams
of sugar per serving

_____ cereal

_____ grams
of sugar per serving

_____ cereal

_____ grams
of sugar per serving

Our Favorite Cereal

Children use tally marks to collect data about favorite cereals and then record this data on a graph.

aterials

@ large chart paper   @ markers
@ 2- by 2-inch paper squares or small self-sticking notes

Getting Ready

Label a large piece of chart paper "Our Favorite Cereal."

What to Do

First, follow these steps to collect the data:

1 Ask children to name their favorite cereal. Record their choices with tally marks on a large chart, like the one at right.

Cereal	Tally	Total
Corn Puffs	III	3
Corn flakes	II	2
Raisin Bran	I	1
Froot Loops	HHH	5
Rice Krispies	II	2
Cheerios	HHH II	7
Alpha-Bits	HHH I	6

2 Ask children to count the number of tally marks made for each cereal choice. Record the total number of tally marks in a column next to the tally marks.

3 Discuss the results of the tally marks. Ask children questions such as, *Which cereal has the greatest number of tally marks? Which cereal has the fewest number of tally marks? Are there any cereals that have an equal number of tally marks?*

Next, follow these steps to graph the tally results:

1 Give each child a small paper square or self-sticking note paper. Have them write their name on the paper.

2 Place each child's paper square on the large prepared graph to make a class graph of the children's favorite cereals, like the one below.

3 Discuss the results of the class graph. Explain how a graph is also used to show how many children like each of the different kinds of cereals. Ask the children comparison questions such as, *Which is the favorite or least favorite cereal? Are the results of the graph the same as the results of the tally marks?*

Favorite Cereal Graph

Number of Children	Corn Puffs	Corn Flakes	Raisin Bran	Froot Loops	Rice Krispies	Cheerios	Alpha-Bits
7						Casie	
6						Ben	Matt
5				Natharial		Lanika	Joeseph
4				Megan		Lisette	Kaitlin
3	Amy			Frankie		Andrea	Seth
2	Jessica	Michael		Mary	Scott	Bryce	Maria
1	Sam	Sarah	Tom	Lindsy	Will	Max	Emily

Cereal Brands

Here's More!

Have older children create a schoolwide favorite cereal graph. Make arrangements with other teachers to have your students survey other classes. Assign small groups of students to visit each class. Have students distribute small paper squares on which the other students can write their favorite cereal. When all of the data is collected, have your students sort the papers by cereal. Then have them glue the papers to a graph large enough to cover a bulletin board. Display the results in the cafeteria for everyone to see.

Cereal Stats

Children sort cereal by attributes and then collect, record, and interpret data about favorite cereals.

aterials

- 2 or more kinds of multi-colored, multi-shaped cereal (such as Trix®, Froot Loops®, or Lucky Charms®)
- Cereal Stats Chart (page 34)
- small paper cups
- pencils
- crayons
- glue

Getting Ready

Give each child a Cereal Stats Chart and a paper cup holding a small amount of cereal.

What to Do

1 Ask children to look at their cereal and think about how they will sort it. Lead them to the conclusion that they can sort the cereal by color and shape, and ask them to begin sorting by attributes.

2 When the children are finished sorting, show them how to label their Cereal Stats Chart with either the different colors or shapes of the cereal.

3 Have children arrange their cereal groups on their chart. First they should place one piece of cereal in each space on the chart. Remind them to keep their groups in a row on their chart.

4 To make a send-home data sheet or a bulletin-board display, let children glue the cereal pieces onto the chart. Remind them that only a little dab of glue will do!

Example of a Cereal Stats Chart sorted by color:

Cereal Stats Chart

Attribute (color or shape)	1	2	3	4	5	6
red	🔴	🔴				
blue	🔵	🔵	🔵	🔵	🔵	
yellow	🟡	🟡	🟡			
green	🟢					

Number of pieces

Here's More!

Provide an opportunity for children to discuss the results. Have children write or dictate a few sentences describing what their cereal chart shows. They can also record the information in their math journals. For example, students may write:

I have 5 blue pieces.
I have more yellow pieces than red pieces.
I have 5 red and yellow pieces altogether.
I have fewer green pieces than blue pieces.
All of my pieces add up to 11.

Cereal Stats Chart

					6
					5
					4
					3
					2
					1

Number of pieces

Attribute (color or shape)

A, B, C and 1, 2, 3

Children estimate, collect, organize, record, and interpret data as they discover how many of each letter are in a box of alphabet-shaped cereal.

aterials

- ℮ alphabet-shaped cereal ℮ large class chart
- ℮ A, B, C and 1, 2, 3 Chart (pages 37–38)
- ℮ a large sheet of bulletin-board paper
- ℮ small paper cups ℮ crayons
- ℮ markers ℮ tape
- ℮ scissors

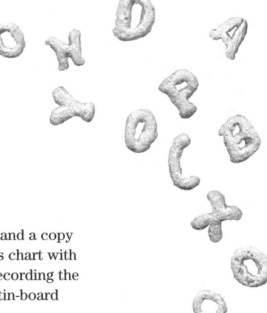

Getting Ready

Give each child a small cup of the alphabet-shaped cereal and a copy of the A, B, C and 1, 2, 3 Chart. Prepare a large A to Z class chart with each letter of the alphabet written on a different line for recording the children's letter predictions. Prepare a large sheet of bulletin-board paper for the A, B, C and 1, 2, 3 Chart.

What to Do

1 Show children a box of alphabet-shaped cereal. Ask them to predict which letter of the alphabet occurs most frequently in the box.

2 Using tally marks, record the children's predictions on the A to Z chart.

3 Have children sort their cereal by placing each piece in the appropriate letter box on their A, B, C and 1, 2, 3 Chart.

Tally of Children's Cereal Predictions

A	卌 卌
B	卌
C	IIII
D	卌
E	I

The Alphabet Tree
by Leo Lionni
(Dragonfly Books,
Alfred A. Knopf,
1968).
This delightful story
shows the letters
peacefully sitting on
leaves until a gust of
wind blows them all
around. A little word
bug and an unusual
caterpillar appear and
show the letters how
to form words and
sentences. After
reading the story,
children can use their
alphabet-shaped
cereal to make words
and even sentences.
Children can create
their own A to Z tally
to record how many of
each letter they used.

4 Ask children to count the total number of spaces for each letter. Have them record the number on the chart under each letter.

5 Have children remove the cereal and color in the corresponding number of spaces for each letter.

6 Show children how to cut along the vertical lines on their chart so that they have a separate strip for each letter. Remind them that each vertical strip represents a different letter.

7 Collect all the letter strips, keeping the letters in separate piles.

8 Tape the ends of the strips for each letter together so that you have an *A* strip, a *B* strip, and so on.

9 Tape each completed letter strip to a large piece of bulletin-board paper. Display the completed chart.

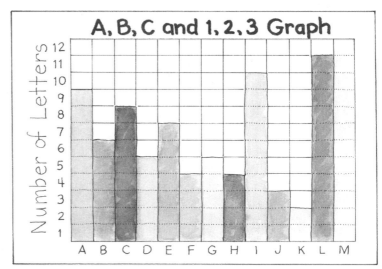

10 Discuss the results of the completed A, B, C and 1, 2, 3 Chart with the children. Ask questions such as, *Which letter occurred most frequently? Are any letters missing? Do any of the letters have the same amount as another letter? Are there more A's than B's? How many C's and D's are there in all? How many more G's than E's are there?* Invite children to write additional questions and answers about the graph in their math journals.

Name _____ Date _____

A, B, C and 1, 2, 3

	A	B	C	D	E	F	G	H	I	J	K	L	M
12													
11													
10													
9													
8													
7													
6													
5													
4													
3													
2													
1													

A, B, C and 1, 2, 3

N O P Q R S T U V W X Y Z

Measure by Measure

Children make cereal rulers and practice
measuring length using nonstandard "cereal units."

aterials

@ a variety of cereals (such as Mini-Wheats®, Puffed Rice®,
  Crispix®, and Cheerios®) @ pencils
@ 10- to 12-inch cardboard strips @ small paper cups
@ Cereal Measuring Chart (page 40) @ glue

Getting Ready

Give each child a small cup of cereal, a cardboard strip, a copy
of the Cereal Measuring Chart, and some glue.

What to Do

1 Have children glue the cereal pieces end to end on their cardboard strip, creating a cereal ruler.

2 Ask children to choose an object in the classroom, such as a
desk, pencil, book, and so on. Have them estimate the object's
length in cereal units. Show them how to record their estimate on their Cereal Measuring Chart.

3 Have students use their cereal ruler
to measure the object. Then they
should record the measurement on
their chart and compare it to their
estimate. How close was the actual
measurement to their estimate?

4 Discuss the results of children's measurements. Help students
understand that measurements will vary due to the different
sizes of cereals used. This explains why a standard unit of
measurement is necessary.

Literature Links

Inch by Inch by Leo
Lionni (Astro-Honor,
Inc., 1962). To keep
from being eaten, a
little inchworm
measures various birds
as he inches his way
out of their sight.

How Big Is a Foot
by Rolf Myller (Dell
Young Yearling, 1962).
A problem arises when
the king wishes to give
the queen a present
that no one has ever
had—a bed! This story
emphasizes the
importance of using
standard units of
measurement. After
reading these stories,
give each child a sheet
of construction paper.
Have each child place
one foot on the paper
and carefully trace
around it. Cut out the
footprints and have
children practice
measuring with them.

Cereal Measuring Chart

Things I measured	Estimate	Actual Measurement
1. desk		
2. pencil		
3.		
4.		
5.		
6.		
7.		
8.		
9.		
10.		

Cereal Math-Scholastic Professional Books

A Handful of Cereal

Children measure the surface area of their hands using nonstandard "cereal units."

Materials

- cereal with similar-sized pieces
- small paper cups
- glue
- construction paper
- pencils

Getting Ready

Give each child a cup full of cereal, a pencil, a sheet of construction paper, and some glue.

What to Do

1 Ask children to trace around their hand on the construction paper.

2 Have children carefully glue the cereal pieces onto their handprint, placing the pieces close together without overlapping them.

3 Invite children to count how many cereal pieces fit in their handprint. Have them record the amount below their handprint.

4 Ask volunteers to tell how many cereal pieces covered their handprint. Write their responses on the chalkboard.

5 Discuss the results. Ask why there are so many different answers when the same kind of cereal was used to cover the handprints. Help children realize that different-sized handprints call for different amounts of cereal pieces to cover them. Also explain that the cereal pieces may not all be the same size. When measuring the surface area of an object, a standard unit of measurement is needed. After the glue has dried on the cereal handprints, arrange them in order from the smallest surface area to the largest surface area.

Literature Links

The Giant Jam Sandwich by John Vernon Lord (Houghton Mifflin Company, 1975). This lively story in verse describes how a town rids itself of four million wasps! The townspeople make a giant strawberry jam sandwich. When the four million wasps smell the jam, they dive into the sandwich and get stuck! After reading this story, have children draw their own giant sandwich and then glue cereal pieces onto it to measure the surface area.

How Many Pieces in the Box?

> Children use a balance scale and multiplication to discover how many pieces of cereal are in a box.

aterials

- cereal with uniformly shaped pieces (such as Rice Krispies®)
- Hundreds Chart (page 43)
- calculator
- small paper cups
- balance scale
- one-ounce weight

What to Do

1 Ask children how they think you could find out how many pieces of cereal are in the box. Help children understand that you can count how many pieces weigh one ounce and then multiply that amount by the number of ounces in the box.

2 Show students the balance scale and a one-ounce weight, and explain how they are used. Place the one-ounce weight on one side of the scale and a small amount of cereal on the other. Continue placing cereal on the scale until it balances.

3 Have a volunteer count how many cereal pieces weigh one ounce. (He or she can use the Hundreds Chart on page 43. Show children how to put one piece of cereal in each square as they count.)

4 Multiply the cereal weight listed on the box (in ounces) by the number of cereal pieces that together weigh one ounce. (A calculator is helpful for this step.) For example, if there are 60 pieces of cereal in one ounce and the box holds eight ounces of cereal, you would multiply 60 x 8. There are approximately 480 pieces in the box.

Literature Links

How Much Is a Million? by David M. Schwartz (Lothrop, Lee & Shepard Books, 1985). This story will help children begin to conceptualize how much a million, billion, and even a trillion is. Ask students how to guess how many boxes of cereal it would take to get one million pieces of cereal.

Hundreds Chart

1	2	3	4	5	6	7	8	9	10
11	12	13	14	15	16	17	18	19	20
21	22	23	24	25	26	27	28	29	30
31	32	33	34	35	36	37	38	39	40
41	42	43	44	45	46	47	48	49	50
51	52	53	54	55	56	57	58	59	60
61	62	63	64	65	66	67	68	69	70
71	72	73	74	75	76	77	78	79	80
81	82	83	84	85	86	87	88	89	90
91	92	93	94	95	96	97	98	99	100

Cereal Math-Scholastic Professional Books

Fill 'Er Up!

Children estimate and find out how much cereal different-sized containers will hold.

Materials

- a variety of cereals (see Teacher Tips on page 45.)
- containers of different sizes
- small paper squares or self-sticking notes

Getting Ready—Activity 1

Fill a variety of different-sized containers with one kind of cereal and carefully count how many pieces will fit in each container. Note: Begin with large cereal pieces, such as bite-sized Shredded Wheat®.

What to Do

1 Place the different-sized containers with cereal on the table for all to see. Choose one container and allow children to view the cereal inside the container.

2 Give each child a small paper square or self-sticking note. Have children estimate and record how many pieces of cereal they think are in the container.

3 Invite children to place their estimates in ascending order on the chalkboard. Discuss the range of the estimates from the lowest to the highest number.

4 Find the mode of the estimates (the most frequently occurring estimate).

5 Brainstorm as a class to decide on a strategy that could be used to count the cereal. For example, the cereal could be counted one piece at a time or grouped by twos, fives, or tens for faster counting.

6 Ask for a volunteer to count the actual number of cereal pieces in the container using the chosen strategy. Have children check to see how close their estimates were to the actual number of pieces counted.

Teacher Tips

Cereal units should be the same size in each container. Cereals such as Cheerios®, Froot Loops®, Apple Jacks®, Shredded Wheat®, Puffed Rice®, and Honey Grahams® are preferable because they contain similar-sized pieces.

Literature Links

Fish Out of Water by Helen Palmer (Random House, 1961). A boy buys a little fish and is told never to feed him too much. But when he gets the fish home, he feeds the fish the whole box of food. The little fish begins to grow and grow and grow. The boy frantically searches for containers that are large enough to hold the fish! As you are reading the story out loud, ask students for suggestions of containers to hold the fish.

7 Repeat the activity using the same cereal placed in a different container.

8 Discuss the results with the children. Ask questions such as, *Why do you think the first container held more (or less) cereal than the second container? Which container do you think would hold the most or the least amount of cereal?*

9 Have children record their observations and conclusions in their math journals.

Getting Ready—Activity 2

Fill several different-sized containers each with a different cereal.

What to Do

1 Have children work in cooperative groups of three or four. Give each group a different-sized container full of cereal.

2 Ask the group to estimate how many pieces of cereal are in their group's container. Have them record their estimate on a small piece of paper or self-sticking note.

3 Have children decide on a strategy before they count the cereal in their container. Ask them to record the amount on a piece of paper without telling any other group what it is.

4 Ask one volunteer from each group to bring their container to the front of the room. Invite the children to estimate which container holds the most cereal pieces. Which holds the fewest? Remember the actual number of cereal pieces is still a secret!

5 Challenge children to arrange the containers from the greatest number of cereal pieces to the fewest number of cereal pieces. Then have each group reveal the actual number of cereal pieces in their container.

6 Discuss the results with the class. How accurate was their estimated order of containers? Explain that even if one container is larger than another, it may not hold more cereal. It all depends on the size of the cereal!

7 Invite children to write about their observations and conclusions in their math journals.

Cereal by the Bowl

Children compare volume as they estimate and discover how much cereal a bowl holds.

aterials

- cereal with similar-sized pieces (such as Fruity Pebbles®)
- 6 cereal bowls
- 6 measuring cups
- 6 pint-sized containers (such as empty cream containers)
- 6 quart-sized containers (such as empty orange juice containers)
- 6 gallon-sized containers (such as empty milk containers)

Getting Ready

Display a cereal bowl, a measuring cup, a pint-sized container, a quart-sized container, and a gallon-sized container.

What to Do

1 Ask children how much cereal the bowl will hold—one pint, one quart, or one gallon?

2 Pour the cereal into the cereal bowl and ask children to think of a way to determine how much cereal is in the bowl.

3 Ask a volunteer to share a strategy for determining how much cereal is in the bowl. Test the strategy to see if it works.

4 Have children work in cooperative groups of four to six members to test their strategies. Give each group a bowl of cereal and a set of measuring containers.

Literature Links

Math Counts: Capacity by Henry Pluckrose (Childrens Press, 1995). This story shows photographs of various-sized containers and explains the use of standard liquid measurements, such as ounces, pints, quarts, gallons, liters, deciliters, and milliliters. The book emphasizes the need for standard measurements and the need to measure exactly. After reading the story, have children use cereal to explore how many pints are in a cup, how many cups are in a quart, and how many quarts are in a gallon.

Money Matters

Children count and add money to "shop" for cereal.

 **Materials**

- money reproducibles (pages 48–49)
- index cards
- markers
- pencils
- glue
- scissors
- construction paper
- empty cereal boxes (You can use a variety of sizes, if desired.)

Getting Ready

On index cards, write different amounts of money ranging from $1 to $5. Place an index card on each cereal box, like a price tag. Photocopy a set of money reproducibles for each student.

What to Do

1 Distribute the paper money data sheets to children. Have them cut out the coins and bills. Review the value of the coins and bills.

2 Show children a box of cereal. Call their attention to the "price" written on the index card. Ask a volunteer to read the price.

3 Explain to children that they are going to shop for a box of cereal. Have children choose a box of cereal to purchase and write the cereal name on their sheet of construction paper.

4 Next, ask children to determine what combination of coins and bills they will need to use to buy the cereal. Have them glue the correct amount onto their construction paper.

5 When the glue has dried, display the money pages and ask children about the dollar and coin combinations they chose. If possible, show examples of how different coin and bill combinations could be used to make the same amounts of money.

6 Have children write in their math journals additional coin and bill combinations that could be used to buy the cereal they "purchased."

Literature Links

The Purse by Kathy Caple (Houghton Mifflin Company, 1986). Katie uses all of her money to buy a purse, and she has to do a variety of jobs around the house to earn more money. After reading the story out loud, invite children to choose and cut out an item that they would like to purchase from a toy catalog. Next, have children cut out enough paper money in order to buy the item. Ask children to glue both the item and the correct amount of money onto construction paper. Make a shopping display using the items.

Money Matters

Money Matters

Edible Word Problems

Children create and solve simple word problems using cereal as manipulatives.

aterials

- any cereal
- small paper cups
- large chart paper
- light-colored construction paper
- pencils
- glue
- stapler
- crayons

Getting Ready

Pour a small amount of cereal in small paper cups.

What to Do

1 Model for children how to create a word problem using pieces of cereal glued onto chart paper. For example:

I have seven Lucky Charms.

7

+

My friend gave me four more.

4

=

How many Lucky Charms do I have in all?

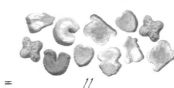

11

2 Ask a volunteer to think of a word problem for you to write on the chart. Write the problem step by step as you glue the cereal pieces next to each step. Have the volunteer solve the problem and write the answer on the chart.

3 Distribute a sheet of construction paper, a cup of cereal, and some glue to each child.

4 Invite each child to think of a word problem. Have children glue the appropriate number of cereal pieces to their pages to illustrate the problem.

5 After the glue is dry, create a display of cereal word problems.

Literature Links

How Many Bugs in a Box? by David A. Carter (Simon and Schuster, 1988). Inside each box are all kinds of bugs for children to count. After reading the story, have children create their own counting book using cereal pieces.

Berry Likely

Children explore the probability of choosing
a certain color of cereal out of the box.

Materials

aterials

- multi-colored, round cereal (such as Cap'n Crunch's All Berries® cereal)
- empty cereal box
- 8 small paper bags   pencils
- Berry Likely Data Sheet (page 53)

Teacher Tips

This activity is designed for older students.

Getting Ready

Place ten red and blue cereal pieces in each of the paper bags—for example, two red pieces and eight blue pieces or five red pieces and five blue pieces. (There are purple pieces, as well, but using two colors will simplify the activity.) Number the bags 1 through 8 and make an answer key of what is in each. Place two pieces of red cereal and eight pieces of blue cereal in the empty cereal box. Write the following statements on the chalkboard: *A Less Likely Chance, A More Likely Chance, An Equal Chance.*

What to Do

1 Have children gather around you so that they can see your demonstration. Show them the box of cereal. Tell them there are only red and blue berries in this box. Ask, *If I reach into the box of cereal, what color berry do you think I will get?*

2 Take a berry out of the box and show it to the class. Write the color of the berry on the chalkboard. Place the berry back in the box. Repeat this step nine more times, recording each of the colors chosen.

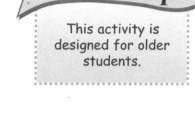

3 After the tenth time, ask children if there is a more likely, a less likely, or an equal chance of getting a red berry or a blue berry. Explain that when there are more of one color than another, the chances of choosing that color are more likely to occur. The chances that you will choose the other color are less likely. If there are the same number of each color, then you have an equal chance of choosing either one.

4 Take all ten pieces of cereal out of the box and show that there are two red berries and eight blue berries. Ask which color you have a more likely chance of choosing. Explain to children that since there are more blue berries, you are more likely to choose a blue berry than a red berry. You are less likely to choose a red berry because there are fewer of them in the box.

5 Have the children work in groups of three or four. Give each group a bag of cereal and a copy of the Berry Likely Data Sheet.

6 Invite children to take turns choosing a berry from the bag, recording the color chosen, and then putting the berry back in the bag. Have each group repeat this process a total of ten times.

7 When they are finished, have them take out the cereal pieces and count the number of each color. Ask them to work together to determine which color they were more likely to choose, red or blue? Remind them that they may have an equal chance of choosing both colors if there are the same number of each color in the bag. Groups can exchange bags and repeat the process.

8 Discuss the "Berry Likely" chances for each of the eight bags. Invite students to write in their math journals about the chances of choosing one color over another.

Berry Likely Data Sheet

Directions:

1. Reach into the bag and remove one berry.
2. Record the color you picked.
3. Place the berry back in the bag.
4. Pass the bag to the next person in your group.
5. Repeat steps 1 through 4 until the data sheet is filled.

Record:

Color of pick 1 _____

Color of pick 2 _____

Color of pick 3 _____

Color of pick 4 _____

Color of pick 5 _____

Color of pick 6 _____

Color of pick 7 _____

Color of pick 8 _____

Color of pick 9 _____

Color of pick 10 _____

Which color berry do you have a **more likely chance** of picking?

_____

Which color berry do you have a **less likely chance** of picking?

_____

Or do you have an **equal chance** of choosing each color berry?

_____

Who Ate the Choco-Bits?

Children use simple logic to solve a cereal mystery!

Materials

@ Who Ate the Choco-Bits? reproducible (page 55)
@ pencils

Getting Ready

Copy the Who Ate the Choco-Bits? data sheet onto a large chart. Give each child a copy of the Who Ate the Choco-Bits? reproducible.

What to Do

1 Tell children that they are going to be detectives and find out who ate the Choco-Bits. Explain that there are four people: Jim, Terace, Ramon, and Amy. Each person ate a different kind of cereal: Choco-Bits, Fruity Pops, Grainy Bran, and Crunchy Munchies.

2 Read the clues together with children. Show children how to mark the data sheet to indicate the information given. Lead them to use a process of elimination as they work through the problem.

3 After discovering who ate the Choco-Bits (Amy), ask students if they could figure out who ate the Choco-Bits by using fewer than five clues.

	Choco-Bits	Fruity Pops	Grainy Bran	Crunchy Munchies
Jim	X	X		X
Terace	X	X	X	
Ramon	X		X	X
Amy		X	X	X

Teacher Tips

This activity is designed for older students.

It is helpful to label empty boxes with each cereal to help students keep track of the different kinds.

Literature Links

Q Is for Duck by Mary Elting and Michael Folsom (Clarion, 1980). Readers can guess why the authors have selected animals for certain letters. Q is for duck because a duck quacks! Play 20 Questions to have children guess cereals by asking questions about their characteristics.

Who Ate the Choco-Bits?

Read the clues below. Then, put X's in the grid to show which cereals each
person did not eat. Can you use the grid to tell who ate the Choco-Bits?
Hint: Each person ate a different cereal.

	Choco-Bits	Fruity Pops	Grainy Bran	Crunchy Munchies
Jim				
Terace				
Ramon				
Amy				

Clues:

1. Jim and Terace did not eat the Fruity Pops.

2. Amy and Terace did not eat the Grainy Bran.

3. Ramon did not eat the Crunchy Munchies.

4. Terace and Ramon did not eat the Choco-Bits.

5. Ramon did not eat the Grainy Bran.

Answer:

_____ **ate the Choco-Bits.**

Cereal Math-Scholastic Professional Books

The New Cereal on the Block

Children invent a recipe for their own cereal using fractions.

aterials

@ The New Cereal on the Block data sheet (page 57)
@ pencils   @ measuring cups (1 cup and 1/4 cup)

Getting Ready

Give each child a copy of the New Cereal on the Block data sheet.

What to Do

1 Explain to children that a cereal company is in the process of making a new cereal and has asked the children for their help.

2 Have children complete The New Cereal on the Block data sheet by circling their choices for the cereal's ingredients.

3 Show children the measuring cups and explain that they are going to write a recipe for one cup of their new cereal. To simplify, have children use 1/4-cup measures of each ingredient. Ask children how many 1/4 cups they will need to make one cup of cereal. Have them write out the recipe in their math journals.

4 Have children describe how the cereal should taste. Then ask them to describe the cereal's shape(s), texture(s), and color(s). Ask children to think of a name for the new cereal.

5 Invite children to design a picture for the box of their cereal. (They will be able to use their picture in the next activity, "Shapely Packaging.")

6 Provide an opportunity for children to share their new cereal creations. Have children write a description of their new cereals in their math journals.

Literature Links

The Toothpaste Millionaire by Jean Merrill (Houghton Mifflin Company, 1972). This chapter book describes how twelve-year-old Rufus Mayflower creates, packages, and markets his own original toothpaste brand.

Name _____ Date _____

The New Cereal on the Block

Ingredients:

strawberries	cherries	grapes	bananas	apples
tomatoes	peas	broccoli	spinach	potatoes
marshmallows	butter	ice cream	eggs	cheese
peanuts	pretzels	potato chips	popcorn	nachos
peanut butter	jelly	maple syrup	honey	jam
vanilla cream	peppermint	bubble gum	fudge	cookies

other: _____

Cereal Shapes:

squares	rectangles	crescent moons	stars	triangles
circles	diamonds	hexagons	ovals	octagons

other: _____

Cereal Texture:

soft	smooth	crunchy	chewy	sticky

other: _____

Cereal Colors:

rainbow colors	red	blue	green	purple
orange	yellow	brown	black	pink

other: _____

This is how the cereal would taste: _____

_____

This is the new name for the cereal: _____

_____

Cereal Math-Scholastic Professional Books

Shapely Packaging

Children create three-dimensional geometric shapes and design cereal packages.

aterials

- geometric blocks
- geometric shapes reproducibles (pages 60–63)
- cereal boxes (include a variety of sizes and a cylindrical oatmeal box)
- scissors   glue   crayons   pencils

Getting Ready

If geometric blocks are not available, cut and assemble geometric shapes on pages 60–63 (cube, rectangular prism, cylinder, and a triangular pyramid.)

What to Do

1 Show children the geometric blocks and ask volunteers to name the shapes.

2 Ask children which shape they think would be best for a cereal package. Explain that stores need to display the cereal, therefore packages that are stackable are preferred.

3 Ask children which geometric shapes are stackable. Have them try to stack their choices. Cylinders, cubes, and rectangular prisms are the most easily stacked shapes.

4 Next, explain to children that companies want appealing and attractive packages to entice shoppers to buy the product. Show children several cereal boxes and discuss the package designs,

Teacher Tips

This is a great follow-up activity to the The New Cereal on the Block. In this activity, you can have children design a package for the cereal they "invented" in the previous activity. This activity can also be done independently of The New Cereal on the Block.

pictures, words, and colors used. Ask children which packages they find appealing and why.

5 Explain to children that they will pretend to be cereal-package designers. They must decide on a shape and design for their package. Recall what they said about the use of colors, words, and pictures.

6 Distribute the geometric pattern sheets to children and have them cut out the shapes.

7 Show children which part will be the cover of their package when it is assembled. Invite them to decorate their packages before they assemble them. (It will be easier for them to write on the packages when they are flat.)

8 When they are finished with their design, children can assemble their packages. Have them fold along the dotted lines. Demonstrate how to glue along the tab edges and assemble the package. Let the glue dry thoroughly.

9 Create a table display of the newly created cereal packages. Invite children to discuss what aspects of the packages make them appealing and effective.

Literature Links

The Secret Birthday Message by Eric Carle (HarperCollins Publishers, 1971). Tim receives a birthday message written with geometric clues. The clues help the boy discover his birthday surprise. After reading the story, take children on a shape hunt. Have them identify various shapes seen around the school. When children return to the room, have them write in their math journals about the different shapes of things they saw. For example: *I saw a door. It was the shape of a rectangle.*

Here's More!

Invite students to make up commercials for their new cereals. Have them perform the commercials for the class, using their cereal packages as props.

Cube Pattern

Cut along the solid lines.
Fold along the dashed lines.
Glue or tape together to form a cube.

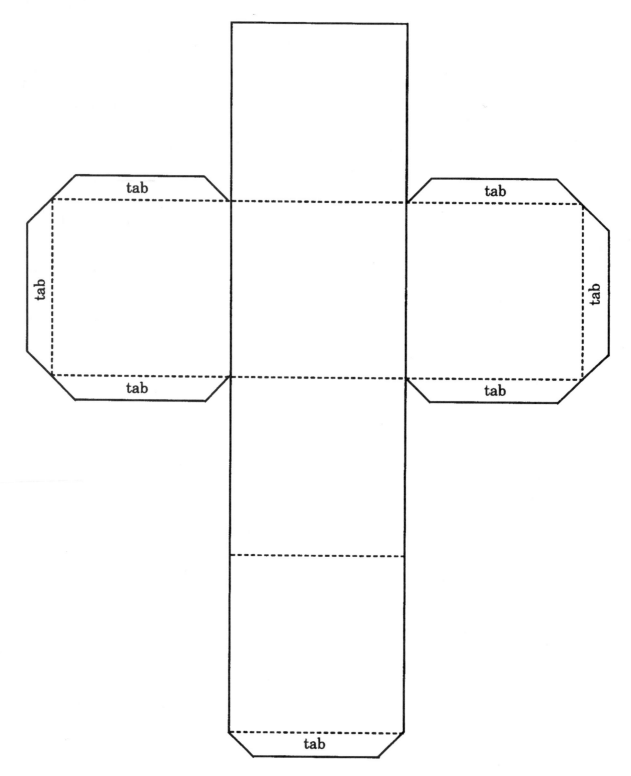

Cereal Math-Scholastic Professional Books

Rectangular Prism Pattern

Cut along the solid lines.
Fold along the dashed lines.
Glue or tape together to form a rectangular prism.

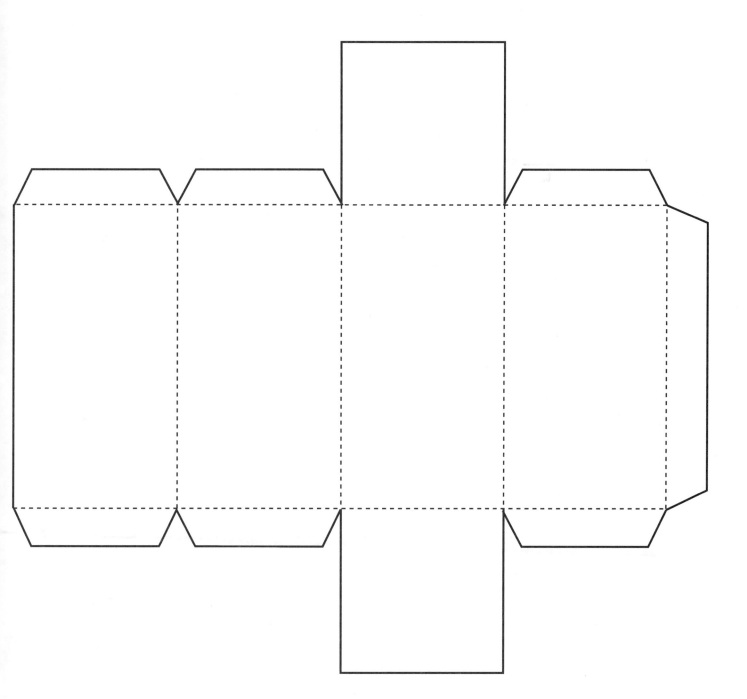

Cylinder Pattern

Cut along the solid lines.
Fold along the dashed lines.
Glue or tape together to form a cylinder.

Cereal Math-Scholastic Professional Book

Triangular Pyramid Pattern

Cut along the solid lines.
Fold the tabs along the dashed lines.
Glue or tape together to form a pyramid.

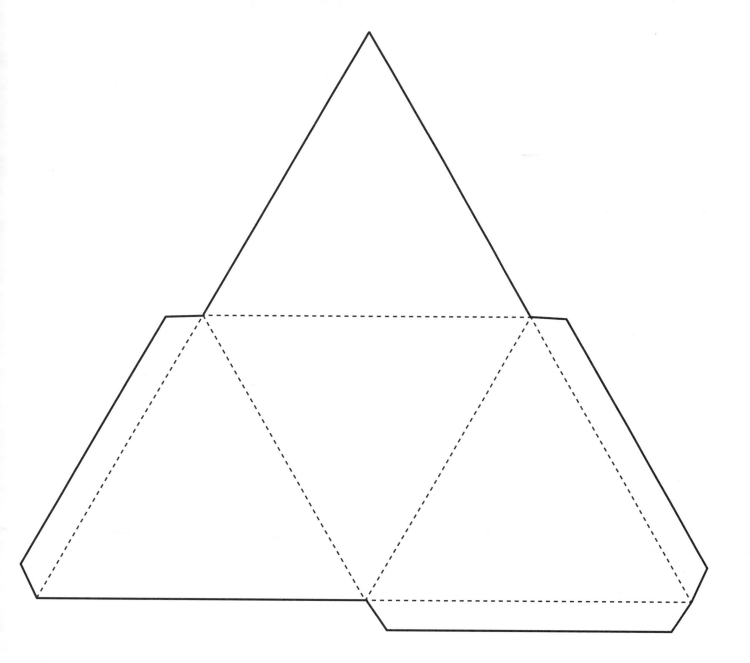

My Math Journal